How to Sell on

AMAZON

Guide Book on Basic and Special Strategies for Making Money by Selling on Amazon

Table of contents

CHAPTER ONE: Understanding the term "Selling on Amazon" for a successful business

CHAPTER TWO: How to Begin Selling On Amazon

CHAPTER THREE: Finding the Products to Sell On Amazon and Listing Them

CHAPTER FOUR: What Is the Fulfillment by Amazon (FBA) Program?

CHAPTER FIVE: Special Tips on How to Maximize On Your Profit by Selling On Amazon

CHAPTER SIX: Misconception Regarding Selling On Amazon

CHAPTER SEVEN: Some of the Frequently Asked Questions Regarding Swelling on Amazon

Conclusion

CHAPTER ONE: Understanding the term "Selling on Amazon" for a successful business

With the desire of providing for the future generation, many people have opted to business to ensure they make more than enough wealth to sustain them and save some for the upcoming generation. For this reason, different people venturing into similar business endeavors, it has led, however, to most the entrepreneurs realizing massive losses. For instance, food products expire before reaching the final consumer since the supply within the market sphere is more than the demand.

Because of this, however, smart firm owners have turned to the different marketing strategies and business platforms available to ensure they beat their business competitor fairly (by making more sales). The competition has become even more interesting following the existence of online media that comes with benefits such as better control of the products, reduced expenses involved, improvement of the customer service delivery and registration of increased sales among several other positive outcomes realized in any business endeavor.

Amazon is one of the online biggest platforms, has made it convenient for the global sellers and buyers. Because of millions of global Amazon subscribers, it is easy for the different product dealers to reach an expanded customer cloud for multiple gains. This can happen in two different ways: **Selling to Amazon** or **Selling on Amazon**. Both the two strategies have their individualized benefits, and hence it is the decision of the seller on which one he or she prefers to the other.

Sell to Amazon is simply an invite program for the Amazon seller account. It entails selling the product directly to Amazon. This means that the developer of the inventory grants Amazon ownership of their list. Such kinds of sales are wholesale in nature. From this point, Amazon acquires the ultimate power to price the product as well as the shipping alternatives. Doing this saves the seller of the marketing, shipping, and advertising of their products.

Sell to Amazon, on the other hand, is the most popular selling options on Amazon.com. The third-party sellers do this selling strategy. Listing of the products is done on the Amazon Marketplace to allow the sellers to sell the goods as the third party sellers. Selling on Amazon is more tiresome compared to the earlier-stated selling to Amazon. However, this strategy awards the seller greater control of their product (control over the shipping, product pricing as well as optionally fulfillment). This also allows the realization of higher margins as well as the power to select from the available two different Amazon's fulfillment services: the Fulfillment by Amazon (FBA) and selling by the help the seller's own fulfillment (FBM).

Considering selection between using of the Sell on Amazon or the Sell to Amazon depends on the user's fulfillment abilities, ROI goals and his or her store among several another variable.

Having known the difference between the two Amazon selling options, this book is mandatory for the third sellers (those lovers of Sell on Amazon). The content of the book also includes the steps as well as the elements involved when switching from **Selling to Amazon** to **Selling on Amazon**. Understanding the term Fulfillment by Amazon is also vital to enable the user to decide on whether he or she would consider it or rather handle his or her individual fulfillment (either by in house or by a service).

The information necessary when finding the product to sell on Amazon is part of the content of this priceless book that will help you enhance your online business. This also includes the principles to be considered when pricing the selected goods for sale. In the case of bulky items that would take a considerable amount of time, it is advisable for the third sellers to set up a store on Amazon. This book, therefore, includes the systematic procedure in setting up such a store for enhanced internet business strategy.

For the benefits of those who have acquired this book, the author has added special tips and tricks to ensure to make more sales on Amazon than any other smart business person using the Amazon platform to compete you for the global market, including the Amazon bestseller list.

Read the whole book to have a grip of the stated myths regarding the idea of selling on Amazon. This information would help you make a sound decision that helps in the realization of increased product sales, as it is the goal of every other entrepreneur.

Based on whichever program a seller chooses to sell their items, Amazon charges them. This also depends, on how much one sells. For the first time sellers on Amazon, I recommend that you consider the "Sell as an Individual" in order to avoid the involved monthly charges. With full information and upon comprehensive consultation, set up the Fulfillment by Amazon (FBA) to your existing Amazon seller account.

For a successful business project, Amazon safeguards the four pillars of Online Marketing Success: relationships, direct response copywriting, content marketing and insists on something worth selling. The four pillars work simultaneously to help the clients have a memorable experience while maximizing on their gains. Consider purchasing this book, therefore, to ensure you have all it takes to be an excellent business figure among the global elites.

CHAPTER TWO: How to Begin Selling On Amazon

Being the largest online retailer in the whole world, Amazon is the ideal market for a goal-oriented product dealer to sell his or her products.

Realization of the benefits involved with this marketplace depends on mastery of the Amazon basics. This information provides clear and easy to understand symbolic status when it comes to selling on Amazon:

1. Understanding the term "Buy Box."

Although the clients click "***offers***" links in order to the available sellers, Buy Box (a CTA button) is the property of Amazon that allows the customer to begin the purchasing process of a product. By considering this option, they add items to their shopping carrier.

Clicking on the ***"offer"*** links (that are located below the product description) while browsing allows the navigator to determine the majority of the sellers available for that particular item.

2. Understanding how Amazon decides who wins the Buy Box the order of the merchant offers list

Getting a grip of how the Buy Box operates is a major step in determining how the different parts of your site are weighted. This is regardless of whether, as a seller, you have ever won the Buy Box.

Because of the fact that there are many different merchants for a similar product, it is important for the sellers to consider the following factors with the quest to realize that they are ranked high on the listing:

❖ Competing offers

In an incidence that there are more sellers, it becomes difficult to climb to the top of the listing. With this in mind, it is advisable for the merchants to shift their attention to those products that are high in demand but limited suppliers.

For faster penetration into the market, therefore, it is advisable to begin by selling the low-competitive items. This as well ranks you higher.

❖ Competitive pricing

To attract more clients to purchase your product, it is recommended that you tag them with low prices. This advice is so because of the fact that most people using Amazon would only go for those items they consider cost-effective. The prices include both the products and the shipping cost.

Regarding this recommendation, however, it is important to offer competitive prices on items that are popular in the market. This will award you good reviews from clients, and hence your ranking would increase as a result.

❖ Merchants' reviews on Amazon

In order to raise the sales a product on any online platform, reviews play important roles to the business persons. As the positive reviews make your business more successful, while the negative reviews end up damaging it. With the desire of securing a top spot on the listing, before deciding to sell on Amazon, therefore, calls for consideration of the clients' tastes in terms of quality and pricing estimations.

❖ History of the merchant as a seller on Amazon

Positive online selling history boosts the merchants when it comes to the listing. Because of this practically proven theory, it is good for the merchants to maintain the drive of upholding the vision and set a goal of the online marketplace.

In addition to the factors above, several others are to be taken consideration of for a more successful online business. Having knowledge of all the variants will help in ensuring that all transactions acquired through Amazon run smoothly at all time.

3. The Fulfillment by Amazon

This program is only available to the third sellers. The program allows the user to send his or her product to one of the different Amazon fulfillment centers for stocking. Having control over the product, customers acquire the product from you. Amazon does shipping, however.

This program gives the beneficiary an opportunity of focusing more on his or her endeavor since it is the responsibility of Amazon to organize for the shipping as well as providing customer services to the lovers of your product. This book handles fulfillment by

Amazon, as an independent topic, in a later chapter of the book for better understanding.

4. Types of merchants that benefit from selling on Amazon

It is also important for the determined merchants to understand the more successful sellers on Amazon. Concerning this, there are three distinct categories of merchants that perform well on Amazon:

5. Merchants that sell niche or hobby products

Because of the fact that Amazon would not start carrying or fulfilling hobby or niche products, merchants who deal with these products are exposed to minimal competition from Amazon. This makes their endeavor more of success.

6. Merchants that sell either the used or the refurbished goods

Since most Amazon visitors would go for the relatively cheap products, they would otherwise prefer the refurbished goods that come with relatively lower prices. Dealers who sell these particular commodities, therefore, tend to be more successful on Amazon.

The refurbished products cannot win the Buy Box spot hence it is impossible for the dealers to win a top spot on the listing.

7. Dealers of unique-to-them goods

Unique-to-them commodities are customized and unique products that are manufactured by a specific company. Merchants dealing with these products become more successful are listed on the top.

Owning a personalized URL store as well as a fully branded website is another way of ensuring you keep to the market competition among the many available merchants selling on Amazon.

Taking into consideration the above-aforementioned determinants is the best strategy to increase the number of positive reviews that would enhance your sales. This methodology is important following the disapproval of merchants paying or rather soliciting for the Seller Account reviews.

Getting started with selling on Amazon Marketplace

Having understood all the vital information required for all Amazon sellers, proper preparation is necessary for a more profiting and reliable business adventure.

1) Preparation of the business information

This preparation includes all the business data, including the basic contact and company facts: A brand name shown to shoppers, the legal business name, a Customer Service phone number and email dress as well as both the bank account and routing numbers.

Detailed and reliable business information allows the buyers to understand the sellers of their goods. The info should include the seller's preferred shipping method as well as the rates.

Both the business account and the seller profile are vital for the every new Amazon Marketplace seller.

Having given a hint of the desired information for the business account, a good and attractive profile must have the following:

- ❖ An attractive logo that has about 120 pixel
- ❖ An about section that provides the facts that define the seller
- ❖ The important return and refund section
- ❖ Privacy policy
- ❖ Information about both the shipping and carriers times included within a shipping information section.

2) Preparation of the product information

For any marketing platform to help you towards your quest of making more sales for your product, it is vital to provide all the required information regarding the product to be sold. This tip is no different when it comes to the Amazon Marketplace.

To qualify for listing, every commodity made accessible to consumers have to include both the Universal Product Code (UPC) and the stock keeping unit (SKU).

Other than the UPC and the SKU, the other information required for increased sales include the following:

- ❖ The product title
- ❖ The image of the product
- ❖ The product's description as well as the specifications
- ❖ List of the search terms or related keywords
- ❖ The product's Amazon category

In case the product is already listed on Amazon, it is recommended that the seller have an Amazon Standard Identification Number (ASIN) for the product. Acquisition of this number allows for the multiplication of the previous sale of the item.

N/B: Amazon only accepts a product description produced in XML, text or via the web-based product submission tool or desktop.

3) Creation of an Amazon Seller Account

With both the business and product description already in place, creating an Amazon seller account is the initial step required before posting the first batch of product for accessibility by the target clients on Amazon.

Once Amazon verifies the account, the posted items would be live after a couple of hours

Setting up an Amazon involve a series of steps that ought to be systematically considered:

1. From the **Amazon homepage**, click on the **Your Account** from the drop-down box. This option is found under your name located on the right-hand side of the Amazon homepage.
2. Upon the selection of the **Your Account** icon, the next step involves tapping on **Your Seller Account**. This option is found near the top of the menu located towards the right column on the page.
3. The third step entails clicking on the **Start Selling** icon. Selecting this option will automatically take you to a new page in order to decide on the type of seller you are. Depending on your desired seller category, select either the **Individual Sellers** category or the **Professional Sellers**. Except the commission levied from each order by Amazon, Individual Sellers do not pay the selling fees.
Professional Sellers, however, is subject to selling fees. These Professional Sellers being fee-based is usually advisable for

consideration by the profitable merchants who own offline stores otherwise.

4. The fourth procedure involved during the starting up of a seller account is to key in the information you consider relevant to the increased sales of the goods you intend to deal with (normally the seller information). Such information can include the credit card information, the business name, billing address among several other vital facts about the endeavor.

5. Verification of the phone number is crucial once all the information is keyed in. To do this, just type your handset number and then tap **Call now**. Upon doing this, you will receive an automated phone call that would provide a four-digit pin that you ought to type it in order to continue with the registration process.

6. To complete the registration process, tap on the **Register and Continue**.

Once your Amazon Account is up to date, you are now ready to list your items to allow them to be accessible to all the global Amazon clients.

Creation of an account is an initial step involved in realizing more profit out of your business endeavor.

CHAPTER THREE: Finding the Products to Sell On Amazon and Listing Them

Now with your account now set up (either the Individual Seller or the Professional Sellers), it is your responsibility as the owner to put it to work. Putting your account to work entails sourcing for the products to sell on Amazon. This sourcing of products is the most vital determinant of the success. Because of this statement, it is an important decision, however, to think about picking the items to sell on Amazon.

Failing to select the most appropriate item would be the beginning of your business failure regardless of finding good prices, quality products, optimized listing as well as the identification of suitable suppliers among several other parameters.

General characteristics of the products to be sold on Amazon for success

In the introductory part of this chapter, information regarding the benefits of considering the benefits that come hand in hand with being selective with the product one desires to sell on Amazon.

However, some important features ought to be considered before investing in the products to sell on the Amazon online platform:

1. The selected product should be lightweight

The shipping cost of a product depends on the overall weight of the item. To support this, most of the products that attract more clients are light in weight to cost them less.

Because of this, it is necessary for the Amazon seller to consider the lightweight products to prepare for multiple profits at the end of the effort. To support the online entrepreneurs, professionals advise that any item that is over 4 pounds is too heavy to score high in the listing. The weight of the products takes into account the item itself, the shipping box as well as the packaging matter.

Determining the exact mass of an item is not easy. Because of this case, merchants should locate similar products with similar properties, including the size of the product on Amazon. From the site, focus on the shipping weight located within the icon **Product Details**.

The weight of an item determines the shipping cost from the supplier of your choice to the Amazon stores. This, therefore, means that the lighter the product, the higher the profit margins.

In addition to its importance in the determination of the shipping cost, it is also vital in the estimation of the Amazon fees. For instance, Amazon charges about $2 for a 2-pound item. Additional masses are charged at $ 0.39 for every pound.

Considering this property would help you in ensuring that you realize more profit compared to your competitors.

2. **The product should have an average sale price ranging from $10 to $50**

Before making an order for any product, it is important for a merchant to have knowledge of the product's price. Research has shown that most people would consider purchasing goods that have prices that range from $10 to $50. People would consider further research on the product unnecessary because they are willing to take the risk of losing the small amount of cash in the case the product is in poor condition. The surplus buying of products with a cost between

$10 and $50 invalidates the initial research because of the cost incurred during the process.

Products with such pocket-friendly cost are simple with no comprehensive parts that are as well delicate and hence special care should be focused on it.

The relatively cheaper products become easier to enter into the market when compared to those products that have prices outside that given range ($10-$50). This easy market entry can as well be because of the fewer dollars that would be spent on the inventory.

Ensure you make higher profits by considering dealing with products that range within the set prices.

3. **Go for at least three products that have less than fifty reviews on the first page.**

Dealing with products that have fewer feedbacks is recommended because such items are considered easy to beat. Having such a commodity means that we would be able to reach the first page when it comes to the listing.

It is, therefore, important for the merchants to go for those listings with 50 or fewer reviews. This consideration would boost the possibility of your products getting an opportunity to the first page; I can't emphasize enough the importance of having your product to appear on the first page.

In your search for a good-looking products, consider one that is high in demand but with fewer reviews.

Experienced marketing professionals argue that the number of reviews an item has can determine the market competition. That is, the lesser the number of reviews, the better the commodity.

4. Go for a good that is simple and is not easily broken

The pride of any seller is when the product he or she is dealing with reaches the end consumer safe. That is, without any reported breakage.

For this reason, most of the successful Amazon sellers decide to deal with the simple items that have greater possibilities of reaching the clients in good states during the shipping period. These smart people ensure this by avoiding commodities that have more than one parts such as the electronics.

Going for generic goodies that are designed for specific purposes is one strategy that online marketers employ to reduce their risks of losing much money in their businesses.

Alternatively, it is good to consider the products you can trace the suppliers.

Items that are considered simple must possess the following characteristics:

- They lack electronic parts
- They do not have moving parts
- Are durable
- Are designed to perform a specific function
- Are easy to operate even in the absence of instructional manuals
- The products are normally generic

You should no longer waste much of your hard-earned cash for the intricate products; simply go for the durable and easy to operate goods that will not inconvenience you before reaching the final consumer.

5. **There should be no brand Names within the Product Niche/category**

The product that an online seller decides to deal with should not compete with any existing brand name. This would mean that a lot of cash would have to be used to ensure that the sale of the commodity reaches the set standard.

This strategy is helpful bearing in mind the characteristic of customers to be selective with specific brands over the others. Going for good that does not have any competing brand would ensure that there is no competition and hence many clients would decide to purchase your items.

To determine whether there is already an existing brand that would compete your item, search your item's keyword in Amazon. In case you identify a product brand in the first page, it is better you avoid dealing with that product and source for other items provided you are sure of making a profit after their sales.

For the new Amazon sellers, it is not advisable to go for products with already existing brands. This advice matters putting in mind that it is not easy to compete with big and common brands that are known by many.

The bad goods, on the other hand, are characterized by the following properties:

- They demand high-quality standards as well as great warranties.
- The goods are fragile and require special care during shipping practices.
- Have multiple sellers that deal with large volume
- The goods are sold at Best Buy or rather the Wal-Mart

Viewing the products to sell on Amazon based on the various properties (but not limited to the above) is the first step that successful Amazon members take to ensure they don't record losses.

Sourcing products to sell on Amazon

In a business setup, a good product is a single profitable item rather than a profitable product niche. To ensure that you harvest much from your investment, therefore, having a complete understanding of what makes a good product is required of you.

Such products have the qualities highlighted in the earlier in the chapter to provide the determined fellows thinking baseline during their business-planning phase.

Selecting the best product to sell requires the following of a systematic procedure to avoid making losses when trying to sell different commodities without surveying the market conditions:

- **Conduct a comprehensive research to find good products to sell on Amazon**

Products sold online are included in different categories for the client to identify them with ease. This strategy makes it favorable for the Amazon sellers to make decisions on the best product to sell.

For this reason, there are different tools that can help you determine the most convenient good: Alibaba, eBay, Amazon, and Etsy among several other tools.

This book, however, is biased to Amazon-based content and hence will primarily focus on the Amazon search tool. One of the fastest means of finding a good to sell is to navigate through the **Amazon Best Sellers List.** This list allows the merchant to find out the top 100 products that are already selling on Amazon and hence triggering the idea of what product to sell.

Professional sellers on Amazon make money through private labeling of a product. The private labeling means that you deal with a product that is already on the market, the only difference is that you slap your individual customized label or packaging. This methodology is far much better than inventing new products into the market because the risks of making losses are minimal.

- **Verification of the products selling on Amazon for their market profitability**

After viewing of all the products that are successfully selling on Amazon under the different categories, you will desire to remove any doubt that the product is profitable enough to sell.

To do this, the **_Jungle Scout_** is a helpful tool that displays the Amazon Best Seller Ranking, analysis of the market competition as well as sales data of the product.

- **Analysis of the competition and hence boosting your confidence that you can sell**

Upon finding the suitable products and verifying its profitable niche and market, competition analysis ensures that you begin your business project with the confidence of completing other products already selling in that same market.

To conduct this study, visit their reviews as well as the product's quality measure. In case the competitor has thousands of reviews, it would be difficult to race them unlike contending the ones with hundreds of reviews.

Consider the Jungle Scout software to help you with the scrutiny of the market competition for your product of choice.

- **Visit other online marketing platforms to identify any private label potential**

After looking at Amazon with the aim of sourcing a suitable good for sale, visiting Alibaba, for example, would help you identify the manufacturers as well as the suppliers that are dealing with the product.

This procedure helps you to confirm that there is a possibility of private labeling that product of your desire. Considering this would also give the merchant the cost approximate for private labeling that product. In addition to this, visiting Alibaba gives a clue that there are some profitable goods that can make you realize outstanding profits out of their sales.

Doing this simply requires that you type the product's keyword and a list of potential manufacturers and suppliers specialized in the product you are interested in. Conversing with both the suppliers and manufacturers would help when deciding on whether to begin dealing with the product or not.

Creating a listing for your item

1. The first step involves login into your already existing Amazon account.
2. From here, search for the item you desire to sell on the website (Amazon.com). Search using the product's keyword, which can be either its name, the product's edition or even a book title. The ISBN, ASIN or UPC can as well be used when conducting the
3. Once you find the product you desire to sell, click **the Sell you're here**

4. From a list of various condition types, select the condition that best reflects the item you need to sell on Amazon. The conditions range from new to collectible to used.

5. Following identification of the favorable condition type, it is required that you include a condition note that comprehensively describes your product to the customers. The information to be included in the note may include your terms of service. Notations such as first class delivery, instructions are not included; few scratches on the front disc are some of the info that can be included in the note.

6. Having let the potential clients know the condition of your exact good, tag a price on it. Regarding this, it is advisable to price your commodities below the Amazon's selling price as well as that of the competing persons.

7. Choose the exact quantity of the commodities you have at hand. For the Individual Sellers, however, the quantity would normally remain at 1.

8. After indicating the number of items you are selling, the next step involves expanding your

shipping zones as well as the methods (other than the standard shipping method).

9. Once all this is set click on **Submit listing** to complete the entire process.

CHAPTER FOUR: What Is the Fulfillment by Amazon (FBA) Program?

For the small business owners, handling the delivery aspect of an eCommerce operation is a nightmare. For this reason, therefore, Amazon relies heavily on a steady stream of independent sellers to encourage multiple profits.

Registering to Amazon, just like mention in the earlier chapter of this book, provides the user with a variety of selection of product categories in order for him or her to set up his or her online store. The stores are based on varying fee structure: Amazon's Professional Sellers sell an unlimited number of products for a flat rate of $39.99 every month. Individual plans, on the other hand, costs the sellers $0.99 for every product sold.

With the account, it is the responsibility of the owner to advertise and promote his or her selling space across the website. To make it easy and convenient for the Amazon members to realize much profits, it is worth considering the Fulfillment by Amazon.

Fulfillment by Amazon, therefore, is an outsourced handling and shipping solution that only the Amazon sellers enjoy. This Amazon program is more convenient to those persons that are more obsessed with the entrepreneurial aspect of your business rather than dealing with the daily operations.

Upon registering with the Amazon FBA program, the beneficiary creates their product listings on Amazon and then prepare their products before shipping them to an Amazon warehouse. Once the products to be sold are at the warehouse, Amazon handles all the routine tasks that are concerned with fulfilling the orders made, including customer service and return services. The registration into FBA simply entails adding it to your already existing account.

Being a Fulfillment by Amazon beneficiary, therefore, means that any time client orders for good, it's Amazon that takes care of locating, packaging, shipping as well as provision of the relevant customer service for the product.

To enjoy this outstanding program, however, the interested parties must uphold the following special consideration:

1. **Using the Fulfillment by Amazon will cost you**

To support the convenience it awards the users; they have to send some money. The payment caters for both the storage and fulfillment services enjoyed by the beneficiaries.

As a part of the fulfillment cost, the account owner will not be required to pay for the shipping outright.

As an advantage enjoyed by the prime customers, an Amazon FBA seller is eligible to enjoy the company's free two-day shipping offer that is only for such customers. This shipment costs neither the Amazon seller nor the customer (the delivery is done within two days).

Both the storage and fulfillment costs would depend, however, on either the size of the product, the quantity in the Amazon warehouse or how often the user fulfills his or her orders.

Another good news with the Fulfillment by Amazon (FBA) is that the seller is able to analyze both his and her income and expenses.

1) Is the FBA, therefore, worth it for the beneficiary?

Before opting to use the FBA services, it is vital that one considers a number of factors (some listed below) to ensure that he or she makes a profit:

- **The product you are selling**

It is true that some of the fees associated with the FBA vary with the product size. The pick and pack-handling fee, however, remains constant. The amount to be paid when using the FBA program would depend primarily on the size of that specific item you want to sell.

In addition to this, the products that sell quickly are greatly recommended for FBA. This recommendation follows the storage fees that are charged for a product. Sending the slow-selling commodities would mean the racking up of the storage fees and hence expensive for the account owner.

- **The quantity of products you sell**

This Amazon FBA program is good and beneficial to the big sellers who are more concerned with the physical storage space. Sending their inventories to

Amazon would provide enough space for them and hence giving them the opportunity to sell more commodities. This, as well, provides the user with the much-needed time to focus on his or her business.

Considering this FBA program, however, would be so beneficial to the small-scale business that desires to become big sellers.

- **It depends on the amount of work force one has**

It becomes so difficult to manage your business until you realize a maximum profit in case of an overabundance of orders but limited work force. FBA would provide, in this case, the much-needed support as long as this is concerned. Fulfilling an item in your office would entail several trips to the post office. This would delay the delivery of the products to the final consumers.

During the busy seasons, it would require the business owner to employ extra employees to meet the demand rate of the products. The extra employees would mean extra cost, and so it is better to consider the Fulfillment by Amazon program to moderate the expenses that the business would incur.

- **How much you value the Amazon's reputation**

Because of the fact that customers would consider purchasing their products from Amazon, the application of the FBA program would depend on the amount of value the sellers have for the reputation of the online company.

This inner value for the platform would drive the account owners to send quality goods that would not disappoint the Amazon clients.

Considering the highlighted points above, it is important to understand your business before opting to add the Fulfillment by Amazon program to your account. This deliberation calls for the in-depth understanding of your invoices and inventory.

2. There is no quota on sales

To remove the misconception that Amazon would require a certain amount every month in order to be part of the Fulfillment by Amazon (FBA) program, FBA allows one to sell thousands or few products every month depending on the demand for the products.

For this reason, Amazon Company is eager to make the FBA program services available to even the small-scale business owners who are not able to move many products.

Whether a small or established business, the FBA program is mandatory for all entrepreneurs in the entire globe.

3. FBA program is not mandatory

This statement means that it is not necessary that you add the FBA program when creating an Amazon seller account. That is, everyone is welcomed to sell his or her products on Amazon without having to use the FBA.

Sellers who have the ability to handle the whole processes of picking, packing, and shipping by themselves. Such merchants decide on this option to save money that would be used when using the FBA program.

Although it is not necessary to register with the program, successful entrepreneurs view the Fulfillment by Amazon as an investment because the service generates positive returns upon registration.

The big sellers ought to add the FBA program to their accounts to provide them enough space to store the items for accessibility by the clients. With this program, Amazon carries out lots of operations hence allowing the business owners to expand their firms for multiple incomes.

4. **The beneficiary has to pay for the shipping of products to the Amazon Fulfillment Centers**

Even though the program covers the shipping cost to the target customers, the seller has to pay when shipping his or her products to the fulfillment centers.

As a relief to their clients, however, Amazon include the *Partnered Carrier options* that ensure that they spend relatively reduced cost to ship the products to Amazon fulfillment centers. To facilitate this program, Amazon-partnered carriers allows Amazon to provide shipping label that the beneficiaries slap on the items box that is sent to the online store. This minimal cost is billed to the user's account as an "inbound Transportation Charge."

To provide the equal services and benefits to all their lovers, Amazon offers the partial truckload as well as the full truckload options with partnered carriers to those with a huge amount of items to be sent to the fulfillment center. The truckload option is only accessible to the customers who possess either a forklift or the dock.

5. The ability to fulfill orders through other channels by the use of FBA

Most of the successful sellers desire to attract many of the global clients. For this reason, they list their great products on various websites, including Amazon.

FBA ensures that Amazon fulfills the orders from several other channels (not limited to Amazon). As an example of the benefits that the FBA users enjoy include a centralized shipping as well as the customer service practices placed on any of the marketing channels globally.

6. The number of items transferred to the fulfillment center in one shipment is not limited

Just as the subheading indicates, Amazon does not include any restrictions on the number of products.

This is a relief to the big sellers who avoid being charged higher with the several smaller shipments as compared to when a large shipment is involved.

7. You can save money by creating your own FBA shipping plan

To avoid the cost that you might incur in case Amazon decides to transfer your products from one warehouse to the other, intelligent merchants request their own shipping plan. For them to be successful, however, they would need to understand the target market.

8. Your FBA account is subject to suspension

Just like any other platform, Amazon has specific regulations that guide the users in enhancing the firm attains its goal of being a global firm. Failure to follow the stated rule, by the sellers, would lead to the account being lost.

Among the following issues that could lead to one losing his or her account, including the following:

> ➢ In cases where a single seller possesses more than one seller account. For those who would

desire to have a second account, it is advisable to seek approval from Amazon.

➢ Upon realization that the owner of the account has been manipulating reviews to attract more clients.

➢ Complaints from many people regarding the quality of your product might cost a seller his or her account.

➢ Violation of the intellectual property laws. The law matches the copyright laws that penalizes individuals who "steal" other people's creative projects. In Amazon, this inappropriate action can cost the seller his or her account.

9. Amazon FBA fees are charged in addition to the commissions

Amazon fulfillment and storage cost is added to the seller's commission expense, he or she owes Amazon a percentage out of his or her sale whether he or she decides to ship on his or her own.

10. Amazon holds the money from sales in escrow

Once a client makes an order for a product upon sending them to the Amazon warehouse, Amazon charges them the price tagged on the item, including any related taxes. The online firm then takes its share of the payment and puts the rest of the money in escrow for some weeks. The money is kept in the escrow as security in case the customer returns the ordered good.

11. It is impossible to avoid the "pick" and "pack" fee

Although deciding to handle and pack the goods to be delivered to the customer would mean that Amazon has less work, the "pick" and "pack" fee cannot, unfortunately, be avoided.

For this reason, it is advisable that you ship the products to Amazon and leave the handling and shipping of the product to the clients.

Some of the outstanding reason as to why everyone should consider the Fulfillment by Amazon (FBA).

Now that you understand the FBA concept, it is worth noting the benefits that users have over the non-users.

Although the benefits are many, below is examples:

- ✓ The FBA program allows Amazon to conduct all the hard and time-consuming work. Once you have sent the products to the Amazon warehouse, Amazon employees would handle and ship the goods to a customer who has made an order. Amazon answers all the questions asked by the customers regarding the product.

- ✓ The user enjoys the privilege of the Amazon elite status. With the program, the users are eligible to Buy Box Eligible, SUPER Saver Shipping as well as the Amazon Prime status. The advanced and high status ensures that conversion rate increases.

- ✓ With the accessible of the FBA program, the seller is able to sell more stuff compared to their competitors. For example, with the Amazon name attached to the user's status, many shoppers are inspired and hence make orders for the products because of the belief in the excellent customer service as well as a speedy delivery.

- ✓ Carrying out business using the FBA is cost effective since the as a seller you only pay for the storage space while Amazon fulfills the orders. Following this shared responsibilities, it is cost-effective and simple to sell online with the help of the FBA program
- ✓ The ability to fulfill orders from several other channels allows the goods to reach a greater cloud of target market cloud. The Multi-Channel Fulfillment allows the business to grow rapidly to realize multiple profits.

CHAPTER FIVE: Special Tips on How to Maximize On Your Profit by Selling On Amazon

Following the desire of most entrepreneurs to compete with their fellows, most of them have turned to online platforms to ensure they reach millions of global customers. One of the most preferred sites includes the Amazon. This conclusion is so following the fifty-five percent figure that all online product searches are first done on Amazon.

Now that almost all the merchants have crowded Amazon, this chapter provides you with the tips that would help you remain at the top when it comes to making sales. Though some of them are obvious, it is advisable that each of them is put into practice for a sustainable online business:

1. **Ensure your capital is constantly in your business**

Availability of capital is one of the important factors that influence the initiation of a practical business idea. Regular reinvestment of your capital is a sure way of compounding your business for a brighter tomorrow.

On the same note, increasing the Amazon FBA business involves replenishing the stock available in the Amazon stores with purchasing additional quality inventory. For this business expansion to be realized, therefore, the withdrawal rate should be minimized or otherwise delayed as long as possible.

This strategy relies on the basis that any business endeavor would grow faster provided there is a higher amount of cash flowing into the business. Delay, therefore, your withdrawing to ensure to pull out greater outputs.

2. Consider taking calculated risks

The wise always say that those who are afraid to take risks will forever be servants to the risk takers. However, different persons view this philosophical statement differently.

Successful persons make use of available opportunities with the aim of achieving outstanding outcomes. For example, a determined entrepreneur would take advantage of the other financial sources for his or her business, including credit card or even a small business loan. This consideration is due to the belief that the initial capital will never be enough to cover all the business transactions.

Giving discounts as well as spending money for advertisement would cost your business. The practices, however, are vital in ensuring that the buyers are motivated, and a long-lasting association is built.

Risk taking has the ability to ensure that your business appears on the Amazon homepage under the #1-product categories ("Hot Deals" and the "New & Noteworthy" categories).

Advertising your business exposes your customers to the products you are dealing with.

3. Market your product outside Amazon

Leading persons away from Amazon with the aim of making business deals is prohibited in the Amazon policy regulations. This ban, however, does not prevent the dealer from marketing his or her Amazon store.

Blogs are writing as well as article writing are some greater ways to provide the relevant content for your target niche at no cost. Making use of other online marketing sites such as the Go Articles, Isnare, and Hubpages to post your articles is advisable due to the ability to link back to your Amazon store.

The wise merchants to retain their customers by attaching a coupon at the bottom of your packing slip.

There are many different ways of marketing your products outside the Amazon online platform without having to violate one of the policy regulations. For example, free shipping, provision of Flash deals as well as a one-time promotion.

4. Shed the stale inventory

A stale inventory is a capital with the inability to be invested in new products or other business ideas. Such capitals are referred to as silent killers in an FBA business due to the two-sided problem of losing money on both opportunity and fees.

Determining the stale inventory is not easy especially for a businessperson dealing with large inventory. A Teikametrics stale inventory analysis feature easily segments the FBA inventory based on the age and suppliers to identify what needs a price adjustment. This would help you to determine the stale inventory.

Liquidating or rather selling the stale inventory at a loss is a way back to the glory days.

5. Ensure timely shipment of the products to customers

Compares that are doing well in the market have different methodologies of enticing their clients. Enticement can be in different ways including delivering the ordered goods on time.

Statistics indicate that slow shipments disgust the customers who in the end up giving negative feedbacks that are a killer for any business. This problem also leads to the risk of losing that particular client.

To avoid your account from being suspended following various negative feedbacks due to late shipments, adding the FBA program into your account would give Amazon the shipment task (Amazon treasures time as a limited resource). The program also guarantees the client (prime members) a two-day shipping for free. This feature attracts more and more customers to view the items in your Amazon store.

6. Always be ready to compete on price

In any other online marketing site, including Amazon, the one and most important factor that makes the merchants different is the prices of the commodities. The price gives the updates on which product a retailer would want to put into the market as well as making the promotion of the specific product.

This advice is more important for the expensive products than for a low-cost product.

7. Getting a Pro Merchant subscription

Upon creation of an Amazon account, the owner is charged up to $0.99 for every item they desire to sell. This makes it extremely expensive in the event of transacting many items.

To curb this challenge of spending much, professionals advise that the beneficiaries get the Pro Merchant Subscription that would mean that they only pay $39.99 without having to pay the usual $0.99 per transaction. Sellers are entitled to list as many items as possible and hence realizing multiple returns.

Having the Amazon Pro Merchant subscription awards you with the following benefits to the Amazon sellers:

- ❖ Enhanced reporting enjoyed by the subscribers of this program makes it easier to manage the Amazon sales.
- ❖ Subscribers have the ability to post items in bulk following a single click instead of listing them one after the other. This property saves the Amazon seller much time that would otherwise be used to list each item.
- ❖ With the Amazon Pro Merchants subscription, the beneficiaries are entitled to access unique listings on Amazon marketplace.
- ❖ Amazon sellers are limited to when it comes to pricing the products that you are listing on Amazon. Subscribers of the Pro Merchant program, however, are allowed to sell even the products with higher prices than the price limit.

8. Consider bundles and multipacks to make money

The Amazon Pro Merchant subscribers have the advantage of listing a bulk of items on Amazon. This property proves to be beneficial in a number of ways:

- You make multiple profits when you sell in bulk because of the fact that the profit on single-item sales ends up as Amazon fees.
- Listing a variety of products prevents competition for the limited market as compared to when a seller is dealing with a single item.

Although this strategy is beneficial to the sellers, it takes much time to produce fruits and so requires patience from the subscribers.

9. Link your credit card to maximize your cash flow

10. Strive to ensure consistent sales

Conduct regular researchers to identify the products that will ensure a constant cash flow. That is, it is advisable for the optimistic dealers to focus more on goods that sell.

11. Uphold the importance of reviews and SEO in your business

In order to ensure that your listings are accessible to the target customers, the Amazon sellers are advised to search for the Amazon's SEO factors to identify the qualities of a good SEO: title, subtitle, description as well as the various questions and answers that would determine how a product rank upon listing. This search also allows merchants to identify the specific keywords used by their customers as well as that used by their competitors.

Positive reviews, as well, ranks your items on the top once you list them. To ensure to this, provide quality goods and services to the clients rather than illegally soliciting them.

12. Determine your unit profitability

Reports indicate that most Amazon sellers waste much time dealing with products that benefit Amazon and Amazon customers at their own expenses.

For this reason, therefore, it is advisable to calculate your unit profitability to ensure that you are engaging in operations that would realize significant cash flow.

13. Strive to decrease inventory errors

In order to win Buy Box, order and inventory accuracy, as well as the fewer customer mishaps (mis-ships, mis-picks or out-of-stocks), are some of the determining factors for winning the Buy Box.

Following the tricks mentioned above, it is the responsibility of every individual Amazon seller to take time and go through the facts in order to ensure that he or she ensures maximum profits.

CHAPTER SIX: Misconception Regarding Selling On Amazon

At a mind blowing pace, Amazon selling platform continues to gain popularity. Learning to be a successful Amazon seller entails an ongoing self-educating effort. That is theories on how the operation is tested, verified and ruled out to ensure that users maximize the profits.

Although they contradict the facts, some of these theories end up being accepted permanently as truths. Because of this, what was once accurate on Amazon might not be the present reality.

Understanding the models is one way that could help the ever-curious Amazon sellers in making sound decisions that would produce them a fortune. Because of the fact that the myths are stopping us from becoming million dollar Amazon sellers, this chapter highlights some of the myths that have remained to be a challenge to the Amazon Seller Account owners. Consideration of these facts is a strategy that would help Amazon meet its goal of reaching the annual sales of $100 billion in the next two years.

Among the myths that could affect the productivity of your online business on Amazon, the following are some of the misconceptions that are ever experienced:

1. Amazon marketplace is already full

Because of the fear of competition, most merchants feel discouraged by the fact that millions of third-party sellers are registered with Amazon. This myth has made it difficult for both the profit-oriented merchants and the Amazon Company.

In order to match the competition, therefore, experienced Amazon dealers advise that the Amazon sellers offer additional customer service operations alongside selling the goods at considerable prices. Sellers that practice such operations get the top spots upon listing their items for customers to access and make an order.

Assume the inappropriate thought and enhance your marketing skills to beat your competitors to the limited market.

2. Selling Fulfillment by Amazon is always the best

This automated handling and shipping of the products once the seller has moved them to the Amazon stores is done for those who have added the FBA program to their already existing account. This has made it attractive to the merchants that lack appropriate shipping department and with no personal warehouse to store their surplus produce.

This program is not recommended, however, for every individual, especially those dealing with single products since the shipping fees, as well as the other FBA program complications, might drain their businesses.

It is, therefore, necessary for the persons registering with the Amazon Seller accounts to weigh their businesses before deciding to upgrade with the FBA for an enhanced industry.

3. Amazon enjoys most of the sales

Over the past years, most of the resellers and retailers have claimed that Amazon has been winning increased sales because of the Buy Box feature (due to efforts by the sellers). To disregard this, however, over 40% of the sales were diverted to the third-party sellers in the year 2015. As Amazon sellers are becoming better marketers, the percentage predicted to continuously grow over the coming years.

4. It is so hard to sell products on Amazon

Most people are afraid of the commitment that follows the listing of items to sell on Amazon (handling, shipping, and provision of additional customer services). For this reason, most of them have opted not to use the ever-growing marketing site to expand their market cloud.

With the introduction of the FBA, fortunately, Amazon has laid down reliable procedures for fulfillment that hands and ships your goods to the target customers. The seller would only need to identify an item and list it on Amazon for the Amazon employees to carry on with the rest of the fulfillment procedures.

5. A seller cannot flourish by selling on Amazon

For some reasons, including the level of education and technology adoption rate, most people have the belief that displaying your goods physically gives you a one-on-one opportunity with your clients and hence quality customer services as compared to selling on Amazon.

To view this argument as a mere myth, owners of the Amazon Seller accounts have tasted the benefits that come with using the platform to make sales. Moreover, for this reason, the number of sales and users have been increasing annually.

6. More reviews translates to increased sales

Good reviews are important for making huge sales in any business. New users have failed to give the marketing method a try because of they feel like their goods would not move due to lack of a single review from a client.

On the contrary, this notion is very incorrect since even the one with thousands of reviews had to begin with a single one. Patience is the key factor in this case. Provide quality goods and services to your first client and let him or her review you positively (this is the starting point to greatness).

7. Simply list your product, and it will be successful regarding sales

Considering what most of the motivational speaker say, it takes the effort to achieve success. This is not different with selling on the Amazon platform. It takes much to tag your product a success on Amazon. For example, listing-optimization using the AMZ Tracker is vital in ensuring that your product ranks high in Amazon.com. It is, therefore, the responsibility of the individual Amazon seller to ensure they rank high for a healthy market competition.

8. Amazon is just like any other website

A number of online websites exist, and for this reason, many people are using them in the entire globe. This has developed ignorance among the addicts o the stage that they no longer consider the developmental importance of each website. Example include Facebook that allows people with friends, Google to find answers to various questions as well as Amazon to purchase quality goods.

Being that Amazon platform is worth $100 billion annually, and with additional service to their clients such as a free 2-day shipping for the Prime-eligible orders, it is considered the king of all the online marketing firms.

Those serious about achieving success in e-commerce should consider selling on Amazon.

9. Being the only private labeled seller means an automatic Buy Box win

For some unclear circumstances, most of the users assume that having a product with a private and unique label would guarantee it a success in the market. This is, however, not the case since research proves the point: reviews beget reviews. It is, therefore, vital for the sellers of a product to maintain high-quality products and services in order to attract positive feedbacks that would drive you towards attaining your goal of making abundant sales.

For new products, fortunately, a testimonial from strangers has proven to be handy in kicking off the sales of the products on a higher note.

10. The lowest price wins the Buy Box

Providing products for lower prices is a temporary marketing strategy that is unnecessary. This policy has been employed by most of the sellers introducing new a new product that has numerous competitors.

To win the Buy Box, however, consider all the factors that are in accordance with the Amazon policies: upholding the quality of both the goods and customer services among several other strategies.

With all the content now in your reach, take time and go through it to eliminate any useless myths that could act as a barrier against you reaching the designated end.

CHAPTER SEVEN: Some of the Frequently Asked Questions Regarding Swelling on Amazon

The content of the earlier chapters includes all the information necessary for better understanding of the principles guiding selling on Amazon. In addition to the already detailed information already included, this chapter includes some of the commonly asked questions that might prove useful for those who find it difficult to read the entire book. The chapter also gives a summary of the key points that led to the development of the book.

Not to waste time, the following are some of the concerns that have repeatedly been raised by the lovers of Amazon as an online marketing platform:

A. What does Selling on Amazon mean?

Selling on Amazon is described as a package that provides the visionary merchants the chance to sell their items as well as their inventory on Amazon.com.

B. Are there specifications when it comes to specific item categories to be sold on Amazon?

Products that are mostly transacted on Amazon include the following categories: Amazon Device Accessories, Musical Instruments, Automotive, Baby Books, Industry & Science, Home Improvement, Lawn & Garden, Office Products, Videos, DVD, Software, Toy and Games, Shoes, Business and Video Games.

On the same note, there are some categories that call for prior approval before they are sold: Clothing, Electronic Accessories, Jewelry, Beer, Wines &Spirits, Health & Personal Care, Personal Care Appliances, Grocery, and Beauty.

Unfortunately, selling Toys & Games during the Christmas season is not allowed. Illegal product or those prohibited by Amazon policy such as guns, illegal drugs, tobacco, and ammunition should not be sold on Amazon.

C. Do I need to possess a website to sell on Amazon?

You do not have to own a website to be able to enjoy begin selling on Amazon marketplace. Upon the completion of the registration process, the new member is qualified to access Amazon's Seller Central platform in order to list his or her new products for sale on Amazon marketplace.

D. What is the procedure involved in the listing of items on Amazon?

Upon registration, the new user can use the company's Web-based interface by listing one item after the other. For the ambitious once, however, upgrade to Professional Sellers to allow them to list their products in bulk.

E. Can I cancel my Professional selling account?

Upon changing your account settings, your Professional Sellers can switch back to an Individual selling plan that allows you to continue listing your items one after the other as an Individual Seller.

F. Is it possible to that I close my account?

Amazon provides a Listing Status property that suspends your listing or even remove all the listings without having to lose your account.

In the case you would, otherwise, decide to close your account permanently, the Seller Support provides assistance after you have removed all your listings as well as resolved all the pending transactions.

G. Are there charges for selling on Amazon?

Listing products on Amazon.in is free of charge. Unfortunately, Amazon cuts a certain amount as a commission to sustain the website upon getting an order for the product stored.

H. How can I manage my orders on Amazon?

For the new discoverers of this useful site, management of orders entails that they use the Manage Order option that is on the Seller Central platform. For those using the Fulfillment by Amazon (FBA), your orders are handled and shipped by Amazon to the respective customers.

I. Am I protected against fraud?

Absolutely. Amazon endeavors to guard against fraudulent orders that might be placed on your items as well as the payment.

J. What is the payment method? How often do you pay?

Upon registration, one of the requirement is your bank account. Seven days after an order, the money is disbursed to your bank without any delay.

K. How am I required to add inventory?

Amazon provides four different methods that can be used for this purpose (submitting product-related info):

➢ Consider using an Excel-based inventory files in order to create different goods simultaneously.

➢ Use of Amazon Marketplace Web Service to upload as well as receive bulk reports

➢ Use the Sell on Amazon button found on Amazon product pages

➢ Use the Add a Product property on the Seller Central in order to create one item at a time.

L. How would I know when I have a sale?

In case you receive an order, Amazon notifies you via your email address or text message. It is up to you (the account owner) to decide on the type of notification you desire.

M. Am I capable of offering a gift-wrap and gift messaging services to my clients on Amazon?

Yes. Amazon includes a Gift Messaging service that allows the clients to write messages for individual products or even the entire orders. A Gift Wrap service feature as well allows the customers to choose and pay for gift-wrapping of each item they order.

N. Is there any person I can talk to regarding Selling on Amazon?

In case you desire to inquire more about the program, compliment or complain about service delivery, contact Amazon's Customer service team.

With issues to do with the accounts, however, contact the seller support team for further assistance.

Highlighted above are some of the commonly asked questions that have made it difficult for some cautious merchants to consider using the platform for an enhanced business programs.

Conclusion

Amazon, just like any other online marketing platform, has provided the ambitious business people a medium to attain their desired goals of an economically stable society. To support them, therefore, Amazon provides two different options: Sell to Amazon (this is where the seller shifts ownership of the item to Amazon for money) and Sell on Amazon (where the seller uses Amazon as a medium to reach their clients while still in possession of the item under sale).

The content of this book, however, focuses on Selling on Amazon for a better understanding of the term, including the definition, how it works and the benefits attached to them.

The process involved in registration is clearly explained in the first chapters of the book. Upon the registration, it is mandatory to source for products to sell on Amazon as well as the listing procedures to ensure you win the Buy Box and hence maximum profit.

The importance of Fulfillment by Amazon program to the Amazon sellers in handling and shipping commodities to the target clients is also looked at in depth. The procedures and qualities to enjoy this program ensure that the explorers and those dealing with large listings benefit abundantly.

Taking into account the current existing competition for the limited market, the book includes content that would help you remain competitive in the phase of the world when it comes to business.

To cater for all categories of readers, the final chapter of this outstanding book include some of the commonly asked questions. Giving honest responses to the questions is mandatory to help the site gain more clients as well as make more sales. Writing this book, for sure, is one strategy towards ensuring this goal is met.

Having understood all the content of this outstanding publication, it is now upon you to grab your copy to remain significant as long as business success is mentioned.

Finally, if you enjoyed this book, please take the time to share your thoughts and post a review on Amazon. It would be greatly appreciated! Thank you and good luck!

www.ingramcontent.com/pod-product-compliance
Lightning Source LLC
Chambersburg PA
CBHW071230220526
45468CB00002B/787